MW00989042

Cultivating a **Pure Heart**

Becoming a Woman of **Discretion**

in a *Sensual World*

Nancy Leigh DeMoss

© 2003 by Nancy Leigh DeMoss
Fourth Printing

Published by Revive Our Hearts
P.O. Box 2000, Niles, MI 49120

ISBN: #0-940110-15-6

Printed in the United States of America

This booklet is excerpted from the chapter "Portrait of a Foolish Woman" in book *Biblical Womanhood in the Home*, Nancy Leigh DeMoss, editor. Copyright © 2002 by Crossway Books, 1300 Crescent Street, Wheaton, IL 60187.

All rights reserved. No part of this publication may be reproduced, stored in a retrieval system, or transmitted in any form or by any means—electronic, mechanical, photocopy, recording, or any other—without the prior written permission of the publisher. The only exception is brief quotations in printed reviews.

Unless otherwise noted, all Bible quotations are taken from the *New International Version.*

*I*f you were asked to list the greatest causes for the breakdown of our homes, what would you suggest? The culture? The media? Entertainment? Secular education? Anti-family laws and public policy? Urban blight? Poverty? Abusive or absentee fathers?

Would your list include foolish women? The more I study the ways of God, the more sobered I am by the incredible influence we as women have in our homes--for better or for worse, for good or for evil. The Scripture puts it this way: *"The wise woman builds her house, but with her own hands the foolish one tears hers down"* (Prov. 14:1). There are two kinds of women in this world--wise and foolish. At any given moment, you and I are either wise or foolish women; whether we realize it or not, we are either building our "house" or we are tearing it down.

Every woman has a "house," an immediate

sphere of influence. If you are married, if you have children, your family is your closest and most important circle of influence. Single women also have a "house"; it encompasses those lives they touch within their extended family, their church, their workplace, and their community. A wise woman is actively involved in building her house on a daily basis, but the foolish woman tears down her house with her own hands.

John Adams, the second president of the United States, recognized the incredible influence of women, not only on their own homes, but on the entire character of a nation:

> *From all that I have read of history and government and human life and manners, I have drawn this conclusion: that the manners of women were the most infallible barometer to ascertain the degree of morality and virtue of a nation. The Jews, the Greeks, the Romans, the Swiss, the Dutch, all lost their public spirit and their republican forms of government when they lost the modesty and domestic virtues of their women.*[1]

The destructive influence of foolish women is readily apparent in the secular world. In recent years we have seen the power of foolish women to tear down and destroy the moral sensitivities and fiber of an entire nation. We can all think of high-profile women--entertainers, politicians, wives of public figures--whose philosophies and lifestyles have wielded an enormous, negative influence on our entire culture.

However, what should trouble us even more is the extent to which foolishness among women has permeated the evangelical church. We have followed the world in redefining what it means to be a woman, as well as what it means to be a man. We have blurred, if not eradicated, the distinctions between feminine and masculine character, behavior, and roles. We have lost our moorings, our sense of what is pure and good, true and right. We have little comprehension of the meaning or importance of such old-fashioned words as *wholesome, modest, discreet,* and *chaste.*

Several years ago I became aware of a situation in which a Christian leader had been involved in inappropriate behavior with a female staff member. When his wife confronted him with her concerns, his response was, "Come on, this is the nineties!" As we have moved into the twenty-first century, there is even greater confusion about such matters. We excuse, tolerate, and justify behavior that would have been unthinkable a generation ago.

At the heart of our current plight is a lack of

clear biblical teaching and thinking about our calling and roles as women. Only by returning to the Scripture and placing our lives under its authority can we be delivered from the foolishness that has caused us to tear down our houses and become wise women who build our homes. What is at stake is not only our own spiritual well-being, but that of our families, our churches, our communities, and even the generations to come.

Those of us who are "older women" have a responsibility to train the next generation of women in the ways of God: to teach them the characteristics of wise and foolish women, to warn them against the dangers and consequences of being foolish, and to instill in them a vision and commitment to be wise women. We also need to teach our sons and young men the difference between wise and foolish women-- what qualities to admire and what qualities to avoid in women.

Proverbs chapter 7 is a technicolor portrait of a foolish woman. The immediate context is that of a father teaching his son how to recognize and be protected from the snare of a foolish woman. However, this passage includes many insights that ought to be an indispensable part of the "curriculum" that we as women master and pass on to the next generation of women.

The first paragraph of the chapter introduces

us to the theme. The younger man is urged to embrace wisdom, so that he may be protected from a particular kind of woman who has set out to ensnare him.

> [1]My son, keep my words, and treasure my commands within you.
>
> [2]Keep my commands and live, And my law as the apple of your eye.
>
> [3]Bind them on your fingers; Write them on the tablet of your heart.
>
> [4]Say to wisdom, "You are my sister," And call understanding your nearest kin,
>
> [5]That they may keep you from the immoral woman, from the seductress who flatters with her words.[2]

The writer warns against becoming entangled with an "immoral" woman. That word is variously translated "loose" (RSV), "adulteress" (NIV), and "strange" (KJV). The word means literally, "to turn aside."[3]

The Song of Solomon describes two kinds of

women. One is like a "wall"; the other is like a "door" (8:9). The woman who is pictured as a wall has built her life on convictions. As a result, she is firm and unyielding to the wrong kinds of advances from men. She has established her life on the truth of God's Word. The other kind of woman is like a door that can be easily swayed. Because her life is not built on biblical convictions, she is vulnerable to temptation and may well become a temptress herself. The woman in Proverbs 7 is a door. She is "loose"; she has "turned aside" from a life of purity and integrity. She is a foolish woman.

Perhaps you are thinking, *I'm not an immoral woman. Proverbs 7 doesn't really relate to me.* I was first encouraged to develop this message for a conference for women who were in full-time Christian ministry. My initial response was, *How could this passage possibly be relevant to those women?*

As I have meditated on this passage, I have come to believe that it is relevant for every Christian woman. First, even in the most respected churches and ministries, there are seductresses--women with adulterous hearts and immoral intent. Any kind of perversion that can be found in the world can also be found in the church today. Just when I think I've heard it all, I become aware of another situation where a

Christian home has been shipwrecked on the shoals of immorality. More times than not, there is a loose, foolish woman involved in the tragedy.

Second, in virtually every group of Christian women, there are those who don't realize they are foolish. They are ignorant about the difference between a wise and foolish woman; they do not understand the basics about personal, moral, and relational purity. They need to be trained in the ways of God and discipled to become wise women.

Third, this passage has relevance even for those women who have a genuine heart for wisdom and of whom it could not be said that they are "loose" or "immoral." Sadly, the vast majority of evangelical women have been subtly influenced by the world in ways they don't even realize. The world's way of thinking has infiltrated and permeated the lifestyles of "committed church members." Although we may not be physically adulterous or promiscuous, most of us have unwittingly adopted some of the characteristics that ultimately could lead to the ruin and downfall of the men around us. When we look at the characteristics of the foolish woman in Proverbs 7, even if we are not loose, immoral women, we must ask the Lord, "Do any of the characteristics of this woman describe me?"

Marks of
the Foolish Woman

The first characteristic given in verse 5 is that she "flatters with her words." Throughout the Scripture, we see the power of the tongue. Our tongues have the power to destroy our homes and the homes of others. Death and life are in the power of the tongue--the ability to destroy and to heal. The loose woman uses her tongue--her words--to seduce and overpower men. The writer comes back to this theme in verse 21: "With her enticing speech she caused him to yield, with her flattering lips she seduced [KJV, forced] him." You might ask, "How can a tiny, little woman force a man to yield to her?" She does it with her tongue.

> *[6]For at the window of my house*
> *I looked through my lattice,*
>
> *[7]And saw among the simple,*
> *I perceived among the youths,*
> *A young man devoid of under*
> *standing . . .*

The author now begins a blow-by-blow description of exactly how this loose, foolish woman preys on a simple, foolish man who lacks wisdom and understanding. This young man lacks judgment and is careless; he is morally unstable, and the foolish woman is going to take advantage of him. (Of course, the man is also responsible for what transpires in this passage, as in any immoral relationship; but our objective at this point is to focus on our responsibility as women.)

> [8] . . . *passing along the street near*
>   *her corner;*
> *And he took the path to her house*
>
> [9]*In the twilight, in the evening,*
> *In the black and dark night.*

Both the young man and the foolish woman make conscious choices that place them in the wrong place at the wrong time. This passage illustrates the importance of staying away from places and situations where the natural instinct would be to do something wrong. This is a valuable principle for every believer, and one that we ought to teach our young people for their spiritual and moral protection.

Three times the point is repeated that this meeting takes place at night. The pair ends up together alone in the dark. Instead of avoiding the potential of wrongdoing, this foolish man makes his way toward the house where there is a woman with whom he will end up in an immoral relationship. Like magnets they are drawn to each other. They both place themselves in a setting (time and place) where they will be more vulnerable to temptation and sin.

This is why it is so important to guard our steps and our choices in the "little things." The places we go, the books and magazines we read, the music we listen to, the entertainment we watch--these things either fuel our flesh (our natural inclinations) or they nurture our spirit. By the time a full-blown immoral relationship has developed, a woman may have emotions she feels she can't control: "I know I shouldn't be involved with this man, but I can't help the way I feel." Chances are, those feelings were stimulated by foolish choices that she justified to herself and others. The foolish woman places herself in places, situations, and relationships where the potential for wrongdoing exists.

> *[10]And there a woman met him,*
> *With the attire of a harlot, and a*
> *crafty heart.*

Notice that this woman is not actually a prostitute, though she exhibits many of the same characteristics. Verse 14 suggests that she is a "church woman." She is religious; she tries to spiritualize her sensuality and immorality with talk about sacrifices and offerings. She is also a married woman (though either single or married women may fit the description). She is not satisfied with the mate God has provided and has expectations and longings that her husband is not fulfilling (see v. 19). Rather than looking to God to fulfill the deepest needs and longings of her heart, she focuses on what she does not have and looks to others to meet those needs. Rather than pouring love, attention, and devotion upon her husband, she invests her heart, energy, and efforts in another man.

The Proverbs 7 woman is not fictitious. She lives today. She is seen in these kinds of letters that I have received from church women (some details have been changed):

I have not loved my husband for a long time, and I am miserable. I had an affair three years ago and ended it to stay with my husband for our three young children's sake. Six months ago I began the affair with the same man and have fallen in love with him. I know this is wrong. He's married also, but I can't imagine life without him.

Do you see the foolishness here? This woman

is married, but rather than pour her efforts into her relationship with her husband, she has invested her heart elsewhere and consequently has fallen in love with another man. Here's another one:

I have struggled with Internet addiction. At one point, I was on my computer up to 15 hours a day. It was my way of escaping my empty, lonely marriage. In the last couple of months, I have curbed my Internet usage. I realized I was neglecting our six children and decided to make some changes. However, I met a wonderful man through a chat room. We've met face to face several times now, and I'm considering leaving my husband for this man.

And another:

My minister and I are very close. Just yesterday, he acknowledged in a counseling session that he was very attracted to me, but he would never act on his desire because he knew that would hurt. Now I feel deeply attracted to him. Help me, Lord, to let go of this, and give me wisdom in setting boundaries. I cut his hair and give him a massage once a month.

Twenty years ago these would have seemed extreme, but not today. I am in churches day after day, week after week, picking up the broken pieces of lives and homes. I often feel like we're dealing with Humpty Dumpty: "All the king's horses and all the king's men cannot put him together again"--save for the grace and power of God. God graciously rescued and restored the woman involved in this last situation, but we need to be teaching women the ways of God on the front end--before they fall into (or cause others to fall into) such traps. Each of these women diverted her attention and affection away from her husband and toward another man, with disastrous consequences.

Verse 10 describes this woman as being dressed "with the attire of a harlot" (the outward manifestation) and having "a crafty heart" (the inward heart that produces the outward manifestation). Our countenance, clothing, choices, and behavior reflect what is in our heart. The heart invariably affects the outward appearance. That is why the foolish woman's dress and her heart are addressed in the same verse.

"With the attire of a harlot . . ." Though this woman is not a harlot, she is dressed like one. Suggestive, seductive clothing is one of the traps she uses to lure the young man. Immodest clothing is a mark of a foolish woman; modest dress is

a mark of a wise, godly woman. Few women today, even in our churches, seem to understand the meaning or importance of modesty. Rather, we have adopted the world's standards and styles. I look around at some gatherings of believers and wonder, *Don't these women realize what they are communicating to men with their dress?* Where are the mothers and mature women who are supposed to be modeling and teaching the meaning of modesty? An outwardly modest appearance reflects a modest and wise heart. Immodest dress suggests a foolish, immoral heart.

"And a crafty heart . . ." The foolish woman is subtle of heart. This speaks of being crafty in her intent. She is wily and has hidden motives. She has set out to ensnare this young man.

> [11]*She was loud and rebellious,*
> *Her feet would not stay at home.*
>
> [12]*At times she was outside,*
> *at times in the open square,*
> *Lurking at every corner.*

The foolish woman has a "loud" or "tumultuous" spirit. Proverbs 9:13 describes her as "clamorous [boisterous]" (NKJV). She does not exercise restraint or self-control. She is stormy and demanding. Her demeanor is in contrast to the meek and quiet spirit that is priceless to God. Not only is she loud, she is also "rebellious" or "stubborn." She is headstrong and defiant against God's law and against the obligation of morality.

"Her feet would not stay at home." She's a gadabout. In contrast to the wise woman, the foolish woman is not content to be a keeper at home. She is not satisfied with where God has put her. One of the things the Feminist Movement has done so successfully is to stir up discontent in women with being homemakers and to convince them that other pursuits can increase their sense of self-worth.

My parents married when my mother was nineteen, and my dad was in his early thirties. They had decided not to have children for their first five years of marriage; however, within five years they had six children. My mother adored my father, as he did her, and she loved serving him and our family. She has commented that she didn't know she was supposed to be unhappy until people told her she shouldn't have to deal with all the demands of their busy household.

Fueling discontent and pushing women out of their homes in search of greater meaning and satisfaction has resulted in off-the-chart stress levels for many women who can no longer survive without pills and therapists. The woman whose life does not center around her home and the well-being of her family and who is constantly darting from one place and one activity to another is more vulnerable to becoming entangled in immoral relationships and is more likely to entice men who are vulnerable themselves. The greatest spiritual, moral, and emotional protection a women will ever experience is found when she is content to stay within her God-appointed sphere. This does not mean that she never leaves her house, but rather that her heart is rooted in her home and that she puts her family's needs above all other interests and pursuits.

> [13]*So she caught him and kissed
>   him;
> With an impudent [shameless,
>   brazen] face she said to him ...*

This is an all-too-familiar picture in our culture, where women have been trained to be the aggressors in relationships with men. Few women today have any concept of what's wrong with being the initiator. Why shouldn't girls call boys? Why shouldn't they ask young men out for dates? They have never been taught the beauty of God's created order. Even our physiological makeup teaches us that God created the man to be the initiator and the woman to be the responder. Satan's way of doing business is to reverse God's plan. We have a responsibility to teach our young men and women the ways of God in these matters.

The foolish woman in this passage approaches her prey with a bold greeting. She throws herself on this man--physically and verbally. She evidences the lack of discretion and restraint that is so common between men and women today. Even in church it is not unusual to see women casually, carelessly throw their arms around men. Such behavior may not have immoral intent, but it is foolish. At best, it pulls down appropriate restraints that ought to exist between men and women; at worst, it can lead to grave sins against God.

> [14]*"I have peace offerings with me;*
> *Today I have paid my vows."*

This foolish woman cloaks her aggressive, flirtatious behavior in spiritual talk. Her religious activity is really a cover-up for her immoral heart. She may be trying to compensate for her guilt by what she does at church. Many women in our churches today are active in ministry and Bible study; they leap from one conference to another. Others may think they are spiritual and sincere, but they are covering up foolish hearts and impure behavior.

Proverbs speaks of a man who *"was almost in all evil in the midst of the congregation and assembly"* (Prov. 5:14, KJV). Even in the midst of church relationships and activities, we can fall into great sin and can lead others into great sin.

> [15]*"So I came out to meet you,*
> *Diligently to seek your face,*
> *And I have found you."*

She builds up this foolish young man's ego; she feeds his need for admiration and makes him feel needed and valued. Whose need for admiration should she be feeding? Her husband's! When she pours admiration on another man, she fuels her discontented feelings about her own husband and intensifies her sense that she is living in an unloving, empty marriage.

> [16]*"I have spread my bed with*
> *tapestry,*
> *Colored coverings of Egyptian*
> *linen.*
>
> [17]*I have perfumed my bed*
> *With myrrh, aloes, and cinnamon."*

This woman is consumed with physical, temporal values rather than that which is enduring. She lures this young man into an inappropriate relationship by describing the sensuous nature of her bedroom. Of course, there would be nothing wrong with creating a romantic atmosphere in her bedroom to satisfy her husband. But it is clearly wrong to do so for a man who is not her husband.

The foolish woman is indiscreet--she talks freely about intimate subjects that should be reserved for conversation with her husband. One of the most disconcerting aspects of various highly-publicized sex scandals in recent years is the open, candid talk about private matters that has been splashed throughout the news media. Explicit sexual language that was once considered inappropriate outside the bedroom has now become part of our everyday vocabulary. Talk show hosts, entertainers, and journalists seem to pride themselves on exploiting and exposing explicit subject matter. The more intimate the subject matter, the more the audience tunes in. We need to teach young women that there are things you don't talk about in mixed company. Indeed, there are personal matters between husbands and wives that should not be discussed even with other women.

¹⁸*"Come, let us take our fill of love*
        until morning;
    Let us delight ourselves with love."

The foolish woman does not understand the
nature of true love. True love is giving, not get-
ting. Someone has said, "Love can always wait
to give, but lust can never wait to get." She is a
taker rather than a giver. She seeks immediate
gratification, in spite of the fact that the delights
of this forbidden fruit will last only "until morn-
ing." She fails to think about the long-term consequences of her choices, and as a result she sets
herself and others up for moral failure. She is
willing to sacrifice her own marriage and integrity, as well as the well-being and future of others,
in order to experience a brief taste of the fruit of
illicit "love."

Are there ways you have sacrificed long-term
gain on the altar of immediate self-gratification?
You might not relate to throwing away your marriage for a night of pleasure with another man.
But perhaps you can relate to spewing out
harsh, angry words that grant some temporary
relief but crush the spirit of your mate or your
child. Perhaps you know what it is to binge on
the food you crave, for the momentary pleasure it
brings. Perhaps you have indulged your resentful
feelings, savoring the thought of hurting the one

who hurt you so deeply. Have you seriously considered the long-term consequences of your foolish choices? Have you counted the cost in terms of your relationship with God and with others?

> [19]*"For my husband is not at home;*
> *He has gone on a long journey;*
>
> [20]*He has taken a bag of money*
> *with him,*
> *And will come home on the*
> *appointed day."*

Her husband is out of town on a business trip, and she thinks no one will know about her secret little sin. But she forgets that there is One who knows everything--*El Roi,* "the God who sees." She forgets that "the eyes of the LORD are everywhere, keeping watch on the wicked and the good" (Prov. 15:3).

What "secret little sins" are we indulging in our lives, in our thoughts, in our private moments? How we need to cultivate the fear of the Lord--that constant, conscious sense that we are always under God's watchful eye, whether we are alone or with others.

This woman is apparently seeking to meet "needs" that aren't being met at home. By focusing on her own needs (in actuality, her desires), she puts herself in a position where she is less motivated and capable of meeting the needs of the one whom God created her to help. She was made to be a helper to her husband, but she can't meet his needs if she is focused on her own.

By way of contrast, Proverbs 31 says of the wise, virtuous woman, "The heart of her husband safely trusts her; so he will have no lack of gain. She does him good and not evil all the days of her life" (vv. 11-12, NKJV). She has a permanent, unconditional commitment to be loyal to her husband and to act in his best interests.

In today's culture, many women have husbands who are away from home--if not literally and physically, then emotionally, relationally, spiritually, or in terms of their time and focus. The greatest test of faithfulness for a married woman is where her heart goes when her husband is "away." Where does the woman's mind stray? Where do her thoughts wander? Is she trustworthy? Is she faithful to God and to her calling in marriage even if he fails to be the man he ought to be?

> *21With her enticing speech she
> caused him to yield,
> With her flattering lips she
> seduced [compelled] him.*

Again, we are reminded of the power of words--flattering, flirtatious, bold, seductive speech. She uses her speech to control. She causes him to yield, just as Delilah used her words to bring Samson under her control. The foolish woman stands in contrast to the wise woman who *"opens her mouth with wisdom, and on her tongue is the law of kindness"* (Prov. 31:26, NKJV). The wise and virtuous woman uses her tongue to speak words of healing, hope, grace, and help.

The Fruit of
the Foolish Woman

$\mathcal{A}$s we come to the end of Proverbs 7, we see the enormous impact of the foolish woman on others, particularly on men:

> [26]*For she has cast down many*
> *wounded,*
> *And all who were slain by her*
> *were strong men.*

Feminists have portrayed women as oppressed victims. That is no doubt true in some settings and cultures. However, those situations, no matter how serious, do not relieve us of responsibility for any ways that *we* may be perpetrators. No failure on the part of men can strip us of accountability for our behavior and for our influence on men, as well as on our entire culture and the next generation.

The foolish woman is an instrument of "cast[ing] down" *many* men. She may do so by means of sexual seduction, as does the woman in Proverbs 7, or she may do so more subtly, by means of discouragement, spiritual pride, or intimidation. I have found that I can walk into a meeting with a group of men and in a matter of moments change the climate of the room by my spirit. Without even saying a word I can discourage or intimidate the men around me.

Sadly, some of the most "spiritual," biblically knowledgeable women in the church are also the most intimidating. Our generation has been blessed with many Bible study opportunities for women, but if our knowledge makes us unteachable or difficult to live with, we are foolish women. I have heard men say in effect, "I can't lead my wife. I can't lead the women in my church. They know too much." Some of these men feel as though they need advanced theological degrees in order to be the spiritual leaders that their wives claim to want. In many cases I believe that is because our spirits have not been teachable and humble. As a result, we end up emasculating the men around us.

One politically correct way that women "cast down" men is by verbally bashing them--making "men jokes" or cutting comments about men. Of course, it is equally inappropriate for men to bash women, but the woman is the glory of man. When we speak words that cut, diminish, and wound--even in jest--we are tearing down those we were intended to lift up.

"She has cast down many wounded, and all who were slain by her were strong men." Notice that the men slain by the foolish woman started out as strong men. As a young woman, the Lord used this passage to impress on my heart that if

I failed to walk as a wise woman, I could be the instrument of *any* man's undoing, no matter how strong he might be. That was a sobering realization to me. Even men who are spiritually mature can be brought down--controlled, wounded, and destroyed--by a foolish woman.

As I read this passage, I find myself wondering how many wounded or strong men I have cast down--perhaps not morally, but spiritually. How many men have I discouraged or intimidated? Our calling with the men God has placed in our lives is to be a cheerleader, to lift up their hands and to pray for them. Yes, they have weaknesses, as do we; but we need to encourage them and pray and trust God to make them mighty men of God. That is our high and holy calling.

> [27]*Her house is the way to hell,*
> *Descending to the chambers of*
> *death.*

The consequences of failing to be wise women are deadly. When we are tempted by the immediate pleasures of speaking too freely, letting our emotions and our tongues run wild, or letting our behavior become careless and unrestrained, we need to consider the long-range consequences of our choices.

Some time ago I received an e-mail from a

woman who had heard me teach on the foolish
woman of Proverbs 7. In this case, the man she
had destroyed was her own husband, who had
now left her for another woman. By her own ad-
mission, her heart had never really been in her
home. She had loved her work more than her family and had failed to fulfill her God-given respon-
sibilities as a wife and mother. Now she was living
with the lethal consequences of her foolishness.

*I am the epitome of the foolish woman you
described. Over and over again, from my
earliest childhood, I've been this foolish,
adulterous woman. I now see the tragic
consequences that have resulted in my
husband and in our marriage. I have also
planted these vicious seeds in our precious
daughter.*

*I have emasculated my husband, because
of my selfish, arrogant, manipulative,
intimidating ways and words. How terribly, terribly wounded he is because of me.*

*I have taken him down to the very core of
Hell itself because of my ungodly, willful
ways. Today he took the wife of another
man to church with him. How could I
have driven such a wonderful man to do*

such a hideous thing before God?

God help me. I see how wrong I've been.
I'm trusting in His Word for healing,
cleansing, and restoration of my vile heart.

God has brought both this woman and her husband to repentance and is restoring their marriage. What a joy to see this once-foolish woman becoming a wise woman of God. My prayer is that God will make me a wise woman who builds her house for His glory.

1. *The Words of John Adams, Second President of the United States: With a Life of Author, Notes and Illustrations, by His Grandson Charles Francis Adams,* Vol. III (Boston: Charles C. Little and James Brown, 1851), p. 171.

2. All quotations from Proverbs 7 in this chapter are taken from the *New King James Version*.

3. *Strong's Exhaustive Concordance* (Grand Rapids, MI: Baker, 1992).

Making It Personal:
Becoming Women of Virtue

The following questions (some for married women, some for married and single) have been designed to help us recognize ways that we may be foolish women, and to encourage us to consider practical ways we can become wise women of virtue.

1. Am I building up my "house"--home, work-place, church--or tearing it down?

2. Am I investing in my marriage? Am I nurturing the heart of my marriage?

3. Do I frequently express admiration and gratitude to my husband?

4. Am I reserving the best of my physical and emotional energy for my family?

5. Am I creating a climate (through words, actions, and attitudes) that makes my husband want to be at home?

6. Am I content to be "at home"? Am I finding my fulfillment through reverencing and serving my husband and family?

7. Do I reserve intimate communication, looks, words, and touch for my husband? Am I giving my emotions, attention, affection to a man other than my husband?

8. Am I meeting my husband's sexual needs?

9. Am I trustworthy? Is there any behavior or relationship I am involved in that I am keeping from my husband? Have I been totally honest with my husband?

10. Does my husband have the freedom to be totally honest with me?

11. Am I taking in sensual thoughts and desires through books, magazines, TV programs, music, or movies that are not morally pure?

12. Have I become a "refuge" for a man who may be struggling in his marriage?

13. Am I looking to a man other than my husband (pastor, counselor, colleague) to be a primary source of counsel or to fill an emotional vacuum in my life?

14. Do I have a more intimate relationship-- physically, emotionally, or spiritually-- with any man than I do with my husband?

15. Does my demeanor tend to be "loud and defiant," or do I communicate a meek, quiet, and submissive spirit?

16. Am I a "wall" or a "door" (Song of Songs 8:9)? Am I a "loose" woman? Do I communicate to the men around me that I am "available"? Does my demeanor invite them to "partake" of intimate parts of my body, soul, or spirit? Do I engage in flirtatious speech, looks, or behavior?

17. Is there anything about my speech, actions, dress, or attitudes that could defraud the men around me?

18. Am I discreet and restrained in the way I talk with men at work? Is my conversation ever loose, crude, or unbecoming for a woman of God? Am I expressing admiration for a man that should more appropriately come from his wife?

19. Does my dress help men to keep their thoughts pure and Christ-centered? Is my dress feminine and modest?

20. Have I erected (and am I maintaining) adequate "hedges" in my relationships with men? What are those hedges?

21. Am I currently in a situation that is (or could become) compromising? Am I in a situation that could appear to others to be compromising?

22. Would my husband, as well as other men and women who know me, say that I am a woman of moral virtue and purity?

23. Have I purposed in my heart to be morally pure? Am I making myself accountable to my husband and to another godly woman for my walk with God and others?

*F*ather, how we thank You for
giving us Your Word to teach us how
to live as wise women in this godless
age. We confess that we have often been
foolish women. Please search our hearts
and show us any foolish ways that You
find, that we may repent and turn
to Christ who is our wisdom and our
righteousness. Deliver us, O God,
from our foolishness. And raise up in
our day a new breed of women--
holy women; women who trust in You;
wise women who will build up their
homes. We surrender ourselves afresh
to You. May our lives bring You glory
and fulfill Your purposes here on this
earth. In Jesus' name, Amen.

Other Resources
from Nancy Leigh DeMoss

BOOKLETS
(Ideal for individual or small group use.)

The Look:
Does God Really Care What I Wear?

Biblical, practical and motivating, The Look
challenges women to discover the Truth
about clothing and modestly. (57 pages)

Singled Out for Him: Embracing the Gift,
the Blessings, and the Challenges of Singleness

Ten practical commitments that are the pathway to true
blessing for every unmarried believer. (76 pages)

Biblical Portrait of Womanhood: Discovering
and Living Out God's Plan for Our Lives

Part One: A series of practical questions designed to help
you discover God's distinctive plan for your life.
Part Two: Evaluate whether your attitudes, words, and
actions are building up or tearing down your home.
(32 pages)

The Attitude of Gratitude:
Developing a Thankful Heart

Experience physical, emotional, and spiritual well-being
by learning to cultivate a grateful heart. (36 pages)

Portrait of a Woman Used by God

Mary, the mother of Jesus, was an ordinary, young woman
whose world was turned upside down by a message sent
from heaven. Her response illustrates many essential
qualities of the kind of woman God chooses and uses to
fulfill His redemptive purposes in our world. (40 pages)

BOOKS

Choosing Forgiveness: Your Journey to Freedom
(224 pages, Hardcover, Moody Publishers)

Learn the liberating biblical solution to resolving life's most painful issues.

Nancy presents us with the key that unlocks the prison we put ourselves in when we hold onto hurts. Her dynamic and scriptural approach, along with dozens of stirring stories and practical examples, will lead you on a pathway to freedom by *choosing forgiveness.*

Study Guide available online at:
www.ReviveOurHearts.com/forgiveness

Revive Our Hearts Trilogy

Experience the Christian life as it was meant to be! In this powerful trilogy, Nancy Leigh DeMoss share the blessings of Brokenness, Surrender, and radical Holiness.

This three book series includes:
> *Brokenness: The Heart God Revives*
> *Surrender: The Heart God Controls*
> *Holiness: The Heart God Purifies*

Now with discussion guides for small group study!
(Also sold separately.)

BOOKS

A Place of Quiet Rest
(246 pages, Moody Publishers)

Looking for peace in your life?

If your life is moving at a frantic pace, and everything you do seems to bring more stress into your life, your quiet time can become the most meaningful time of your day.

Learn:
- How to get spiritually refreshed every day.
- Practical ways to make your quiet time come alive.
- How to deal with obstacles to your time with God.
- How to find peace in the midst of the storm.

"Devotion to the Lord Jesus. Want it? Rather, do you want Him? This book is a splendid guide." -- Joni Eareckson Tada

A 30-Day Walk With God in the Psalms
(192 pages, Moody Publishers)

Would you like to develop a meaningful daily quiet time? This book will help you get started. This 30-day journal companion tool to *A Place of Quiet Rest* can be used by anyone, at any time to draw closer to your Heavenly Father.
Perfect for individual or group study.

Psalms From the Heart

This inspirational recording is a companion tool to *A 30-Day Walk With God in the Psalms* featuring Nancy Leigh DeMoss reading selected Psalms with musical background. It will enhance your personal quiet time and enable you to meditate on the Word of God throughout the day.

Available on CD

Lies Women Believe:
And the Truth that Sets Them Free!
(285 pages, Moody Publishers)

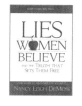

"God can't forgive what I've done."
"I cannot walk in consistent victory over sin."
"I can't control my emotions."
"I don't have time to do everything I'm supposed to do."
"If my circumstances were different, I'd be different."

Have you ever found yourself thinking these kinds of thoughts? With courage and compassion, Nancy helps women see how they may have been deceived. She exposes forty lies commonly believed by Christian women--lies about God, sin, priorities, marriage and family, emotions, and more.

This penetrating book will help you learn how to counter and overcome Satan's deceptions with the most powerful weapon of all--God's truth!

"You will know the truth, and the truth will set you free!" John 8:32

The Companion Guide to Lies Women Believe
(128 pages, Moody Publishers)

A Life-Changing Study for Groups or Individuals

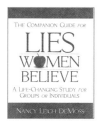

This 10-week companion study to *Lies Women Believe* is ideal for a Bible study group, Sunday school class, or a small group of women.

Go deeper into God's Word, walk more fully in His Grace and experience the joy of the abundant life Christ promised.

To order, call **1-800-569-5959** or visit **www.ReviveOurHearts.com**

To order these or other revival-oriented resources, contact:

Revive Our Hearts
P.O. Box 2000, Niles, MI 49120
800-569-5959 • www.ReviveOurHearts.com